MW00895950

If found, please return to:
SIEFERT ELEMENTARY SCHOOL LIBRARY
24125 26 Mile Road
Ray, MI 48096
Phone: 810-749-3401

Countries of the World

Norway

by Kathleen W. Deady

Consultant:
Ole Øveraas
Consul
Royal Norwegian Consulate General

Bridgestone Books
an imprint of Capstone Press
Mankato, Minnesota

948.1
Dea
- Bridgestone - 3-31-03 - $15.95

Bridgestone Books are published by Capstone Press
151 Good Counsel Drive, P.O. Box 669, Mankato, Minnesota 56002
http://www.capstone-press.com

Copyright © 2002 by Capstone Press. All rights reserved.
No part of this book may be reproduced without written permission from
the publisher. The publisher takes no responsibility for the use of any of
the materials or methods described in this book, nor for the products thereof.
Printed in the United States of America.

Library of Congress Cataloging-in-Publication Data
Deady, Kathleen W.
    Norway/by Kathleen W. Deady.
    p. cm.—(Countries of the world)
    Includes bibliographical references and index.
    ISBN 0-7368-0943-0
    1. Norway—Juvenile literature. [1. Norway.] I. Title. II. Countries of the world (Mankato,
        Minn.).
DL409 .D43 2002
948.1—dc21   00-012529

Summary: Discusses the landscape, culture, food, animals, sports, and holidays of Norway.

Editorial Credits

Erika Mikkelson, editor; Karen Risch, product planning editor; Linda Clavel, cover designer
    and illustrator; Jeff Anderson, photo researcher

Photo Credits

Dave G. Houser/Houserstock, 8, 16
Joan Berman, 10
One Mile Up, Inc., 5 (top)
Tom Stack/Tom Stack & Associates, 6
TRIP/GV Press, 18, 20
Unicorn Stock Photos/Jeff Greenberg, cover; Florent Flipper, 12
Visuals Unlimited/Charles Preitner, 14

If found, please return to:
SIEFERT ELEMENTARY SCHOOL LIBRARY
24125 26 Mile Road
Ray, MI 48096
Phone: 810-749-3401

1 2 3 4 5 6 07 06 05 04 03 02

Table of Contents

Fast Facts. 4
Maps 4
Flag 5
Currency 5

The Land 7
Life at Home 9
Going to School 11
Norwegian Food 13
Clothing 15
Animals 17
Sports and Recreation 19
Holidays and Celebrations 21

Hands On: Fox and Geese 22
Learn to Speak Norwegian 23
Words to Know 23
Read More 24
Useful Addresses and Internet Sites 24
Index 24

Fast Facts

Name: Kingdom of Norway

Capital: Oslo

Population: Almost 4.5 million

Language: Norwegian

Religion: Mostly Evangelical Lutheran Church of Norway

Size: 125,181 square miles (324,220 square kilometers)
Norway is a little larger than the U.S. state of New Mexico.

Crops: Barley, potatoes, oats, wheat, rye

Maps

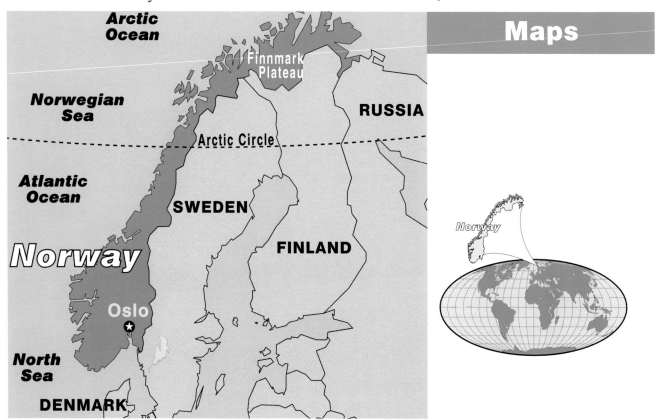

Arctic Ocean

Finnmark Plateau

Norwegian Sea

RUSSIA

Arctic Circle

Atlantic Ocean

SWEDEN

FINLAND

Norway

Oslo

North Sea

DENMARK

Norway

Flag

Before 1814, Norway was part of Denmark. The Danish flag is red with a white cross. In 1814, Norway broke away from Denmark. Norway added a smaller blue cross inside the white cross. This new flag became the Norwegian national flag in 1898. The red, white, and blue colors on Norway's flag represent freedom.

Currency

The unit of currency in Norway is the krone. One hundred øre equal one krone.

In the early 2000s, 9 kroner equaled 1 U.S. dollar. About 6 kroner equaled 1 Canadian dollar.

The Land

Norway is a long, narrow country in northwestern Europe. The Arctic Ocean and the Norwegian Sea are to the north and west. The Atlantic Ocean also lies to the west of Norway. Sweden is east of Norway. Finland and Russia are to the east. Denmark lies to the south across the North Sea.

Northern Norway is above the Arctic Circle. This part of Norway is called the Land of the Midnight Sun. The sun does not set from mid-May through July. The sun never rises in December and most of January.

Mountains cover most of Norway. Many of these mountains were smoothed and rounded by glaciers. These huge masses of slowly moving ice formed many lakes and deep valleys.

Fjords line Norway's rocky coastline. These narrow inlets of water cut far inland. They form one of the most jagged coastlines in the world.

Geiranger fjord is nearly 10 miles (16 kilometers) long.

Life at Home

About three-fourths of Norwegians live in cities. Many people live in tall apartment buildings. Some people live in townhouses. These houses are joined together in rows.

About one-fourth of Norwegians live in rural areas. A few farmhouses have traditional sod roofs. People place a thick layer of grass in rows on the roof. Goats sometimes climb onto the roofs and eat the grass.

Norwegians build homes of wood or stone. Many people paint their houses bright colors. Most homes have windows with three layers of glass. These layers keep the houses warm but still let in light. Many Norwegians heat their homes with electricity. A few use large iron or tile stoves.

Families enjoy time at home. They visit friends in the evenings. Many families own or rent cottages on the coast or in the mountains. They often visit their cottages on weekends.

Colorful homes line the streets in Tromsø, Norway.

Going to School

Education is important in Norway. Nearly everyone can read and write. Schools run by the government are free. Norway has a few private schools.

Norwegian children must attend school from ages 6 to 16. Primary school is grades one through four. Grades five through seven are middle school. Lower secondary school includes grades eight through ten.

Students study social studies, math, science, and Norwegian. They must learn English and another language. Students also study religion, music, and physical education.

Most students attend upper secondary school for three more years. They may take classes to prepare for a college or a university. Some upper secondary students receive training for a job. They can take classes in computers, agriculture, and other fields.

Students learn sports such as soccer in physical education classes.

If found, please return to:
DeWITT ELEMENTARY SCHOOL LIBRARY
24125 26 Mile Road
Ray, MI 48096
Phone 810-749-5651

Norwegian Food

Norwegians eat four or more meals each day. Breakfast usually is cereal and a smørbrød (SMUR-brud). This open-faced sandwich may include jam, salmon, meat, or cheese. Norwegians also eat sandwiches for lunch and evening snacks.

The main meal is called middag (mid-DAHG). Middag is a hot meal between 4:00 and 6:00 in the evening. It usually includes soup, meat, fish, potatoes, and vegetables. Meatballs with potatoes and gravy are common. A mutton and cabbage stew called fårikål (fawr-EE-kawl) also is popular.

Seafood is plentiful. Many people eat smoked salmon called røkelaks (RUH-kuh-lahks). Aged trout called rakørret (RAHK-uhr-ruht) also is common. Both dishes have a strong flavor.

Dessert may be a cream pudding called rømmegrøt (RUH-muh-gruhrt). Fresh berries and fruit soup are other favorite desserts.

Breakfast often includes meat, fruit, and cereal.

Clothing

Norwegians' everyday clothing looks like that of North Americans. It is modern and warm.

Norwegians often wear traditional clothing for special events. These events include weddings and national and local holidays. Norwegians call their traditional costume a bunad (BOO-nahd).

Men wear dark knee-length pants and white shirts. Their costume includes long stockings and shoes with silver buckles. They wear colorful vests or jackets with fancy buttons.

Women wear jumpers as part of their costume. These dresses often are red or blue. Women wear white blouses with a high collar underneath the jumpers. Long aprons go over the skirts. Some women tie scarves around their heads.

Bunads vary throughout Norway. People sew fancy designs on their costumes. This kind of needlework is called embroidery. Clothing also may have special beaded designs.

People wear bunads during festivals and celebrations.

Animals

Many animals live in Norway. Reindeer roam Norway's mountains. Polar foxes, hares, and lemmings live in northern mountains. Otters and martens are common in the south and southeast. Beavers, badgers, and moose live throughout Norway.

Some animals are becoming less common in Norway. Polar bears live only on the island of Svalbard. Wolves, wolverines, and lynxes make their homes in a few areas of Norway. Brown bears also are rare in Norway.

Many kinds of birds live in Norway. Kittiwakes, puffins, and guillemots nest high on cliffs. Partridges and grouse live in forests. Lakes and marshes are home to cranes, swans, and ducks.

Many animals swim in Norwegian waters. Trout, salmon, and pike swim in lakes and rivers. Cod, shrimp, and seals live near the coast. Mackerel and sardines thrive in deeper waters.

Reindeer have thick fur to protect them from Norway's cold weather.

Sports and Recreation

Norwegians enjoy many activities. They especially like winter sports. Norway is famous for both cross-country and downhill skiing.

Ski jumping and skating are popular outdoor sports. Both skiers and speed skaters from Norway have won many medals in the Winter Olympics.

Norwegians also enjoy bandy. Bandy is a fast sport similar to ice hockey. Players use curved sticks to hit a ball. The game is played on a soccer-sized field.

Dogsled racing is common in Norway. Dogsled racers cross the Finnmark Plateau during the Finnmark Race.

Soccer is a popular summer sport. Norwegians call soccer football. Norwegian teams often play in the World Cup competition. The Norwegian women's team won the Women's World Cup in 1995. They won an Olympic gold medal in 2000.

Skiing is Norway's national sport.

Holidays and Celebrations

May 17 is Constitution Day. Norway adopted its constitution on this day in 1814. Norwegians dress in bunads. They sing and wave flags as they parade through the streets. Children parade by the Royal Palace in Oslo. The king of Norway waves to them from a balcony.

Midsummer's Eve is June 23. It is the longest day of the year. People build bonfires along lakes, rivers, and fjords. They eat special foods and dance all night.

Christmas is Norway's major winter holiday. Norwegians decorate Christmas trees with candles, straw ornaments, and flags. People hang paper baskets filled with candy and nuts on the lower branches.

Norwegian families celebrate Christmas Eve together. They eat a large meal. Children listen to stories about Santa Claus. Norwegians call Santa Claus by the name Julenissen.

Norwegians celebrate Constitution Day on May 17.

Hands On: Fox and Geese

Fox and Geese is a popular Norwegian game. There are many games similar to Fox and Geese around the world. These games have different names in each country.

What You Need

2 players
18 playing pieces
  (coins or buttons, 17 the same, 1 different)
Paper
Marker

What You Do

1. Make a gameboard. Draw lines on a piece of paper as shown in the diagram.
2. One player is the fox. The other player is the geese.
3. Place the pieces on the board as shown. One piece is the fox. The rest of the pieces are geese.
4. The fox goes first. The fox can move along a line in any direction. The fox tries to capture the geese. The fox jumps over the geese to capture them. The fox must land in an empty space.
5. The geese may move in all directions except backward. But the geese may not jump over the fox or other geese. The geese try to surround the fox. They block the fox so it cannot move.
6. The fox can win the game two ways. The fox can capture enough geese so they cannot surround it. The fox also can force the geese to the other side of the board. The geese cannot turn around. They will be trapped.
7. Geese can win the game one way. They must corner the fox and surround it. The fox will not be able to move.

Learn to Speak Norwegian

Yes	Ja	(YAH)
No	Nei	(NAY)
Hello	God dag	(goo-DAHG)
Good-bye	Adjø	(ah-DYU)
Thank you	Tusen takk	(TEWS-sehn TAHK)
You are welcome	Vær så god	(VEHR SOH GOO)
Excuse me	Unnskyld	(EWN-shewl)

Words to Know

balcony (BAL-kuh-nee)—a platform with railings that is on the outside of a building

fjord (FYORD)—a long narrow inlet of the ocean between high cliffs; glaciers formed fjords.

glacier (GLAY-shur)—a huge mass of slowly moving ice

inlet (IN-let)—a narrow bay of water that juts inland

jumper (JUHM-pur)—a sleeveless dress worn over a blouse

lemming (LEM-ming)—a small rodent with a short tail

marten (MAR-ten)—a weasel-like animal

mutton (MUHT-uhn)—meat from a sheep

sod (SOD)—the top layer of soil and the grass attached to it

tradition (truh-DISH-uhn)—a custom, an idea, or a belief that is passed down from one generation to the next

Read More

Kopka, Deborah L. *Norway.* Globe-Trotters Club. Minneapolis: Carolrhoda Books, 2001.

Thoennes Keller, Kristin. *Christmas in Norway.* Christmas Around the World. New York: Hilltop Books, 1999.

Useful Addresses and Internet Sites

Royal Norwegian Embassy
Royal Bank Centre
90 Sparks Street Suite 532
Ottawa, ON K1P 5B4
Canada

Royal Norwegian Embassy
2720 34th Street NW
Washington, DC 20008

CIA World Factbook 2000—Norway
http://www.odci.gov/cia/publications/factbook/geos/no.html
Facts About Norway
http://www.vg.no/vg/norway/
Norway
http://www.norway.org

Index

Arctic Circle, 7
bandy, 19
bunad, 15, 21
Christmas, 21
dogsled racing, 19
fårikål, 13

fjords, 7, 21
glaciers, 7
Julenissen, 21
reindeer, 17
Royal Palace, 21
soccer, 19

If found, please return to:

RICHART ELEMENTARY SCHOOL LIBRARY
24125 25 Mile Road
Ray, MI 48096
Phone: 810-749-3401